Paa Ruwi

The Lion-Sphinx

The Carcass Mountain

Paa Ruwty The-Lion-Sphinx
The Carcass Mountain

First publication December 2011 by Alpha Wann
With the services of:
TamaRe House Publishers
www.tamarehouse.co.uk
info@tamarehouse.com
044 (0)844 357 2592

Illustrated by Amidou Badji and Dennis Brown

This publication employs acid free paper and meets all ANSI standards for archival quality paper.

Copyright © 2011 Alpha Wann

All rights are reserved. No part of this book are to be reprinted, copied or stored in retrieval systems of any type, except by written permission from the Author. Parts of this book may however be used only in reference to support related documents or subjects.

A CIP record for this title is available from the British Library.

ISBN 978-1-908552-13-6

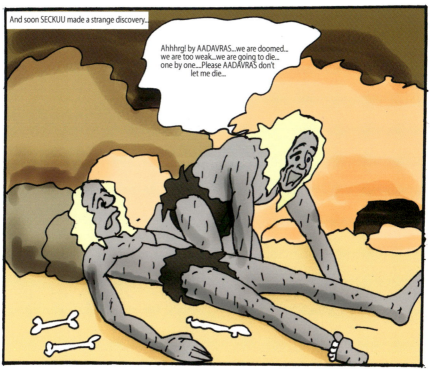

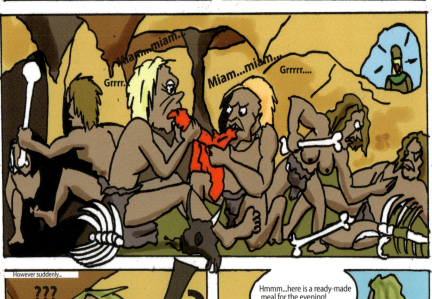

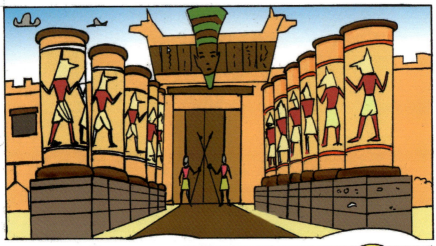
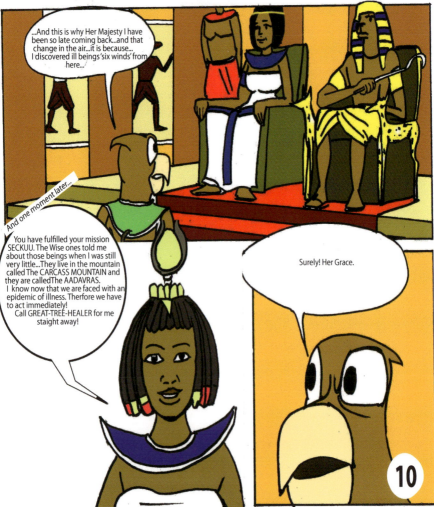

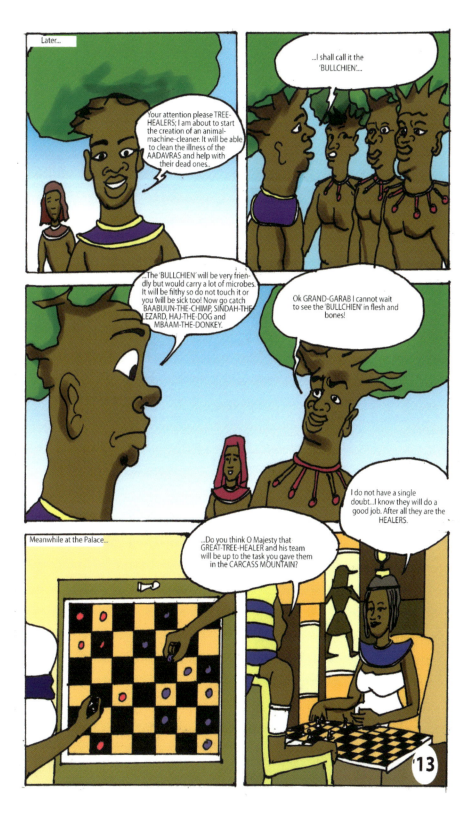

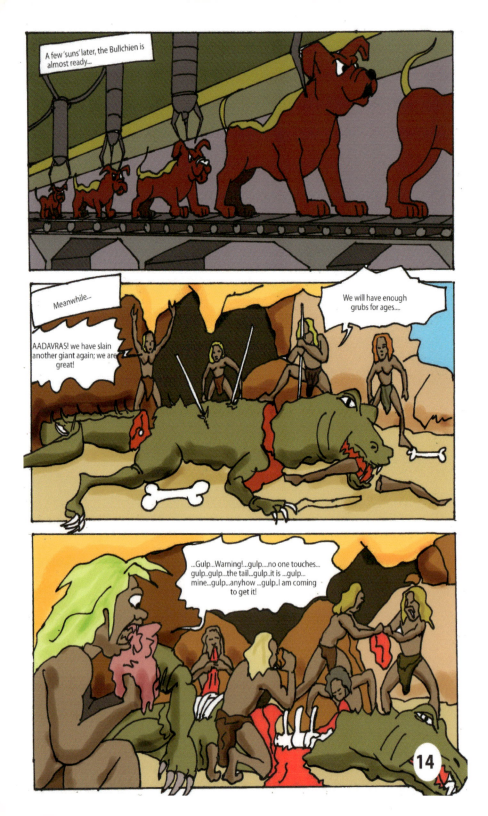

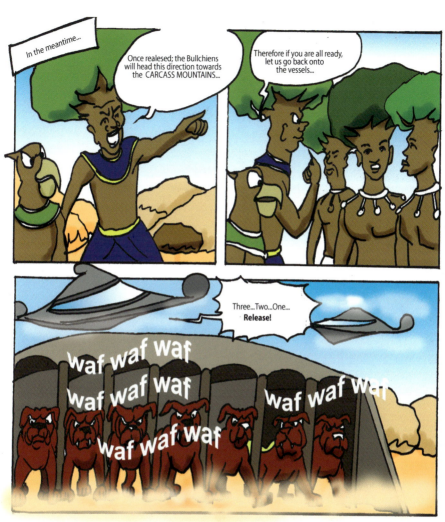

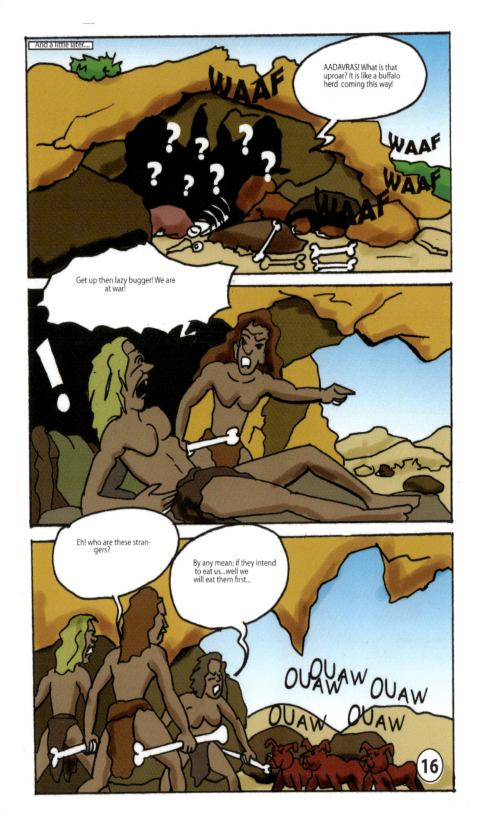

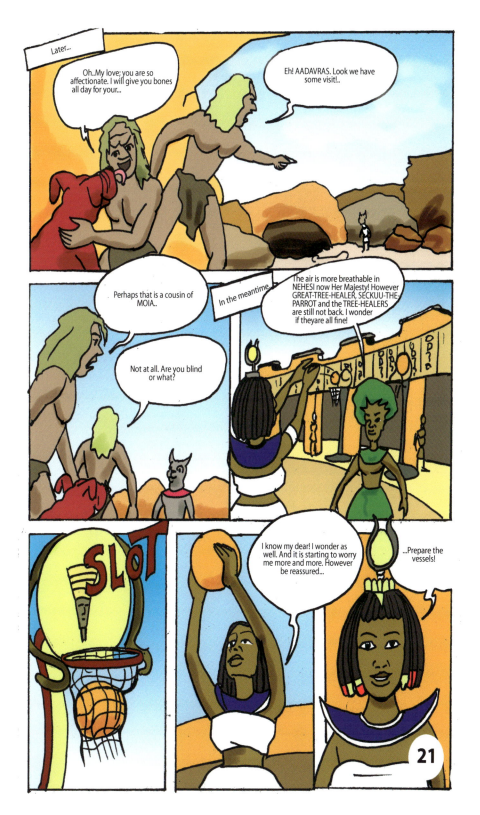

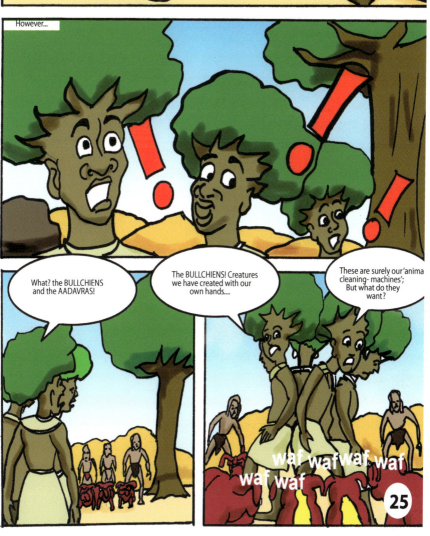

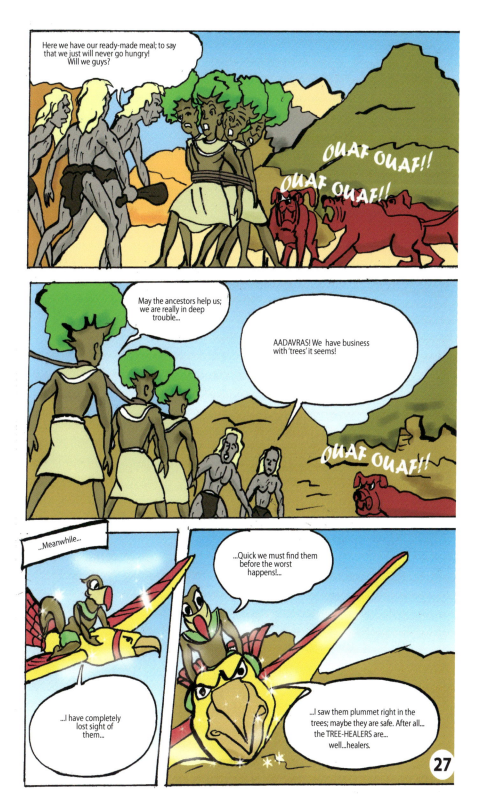

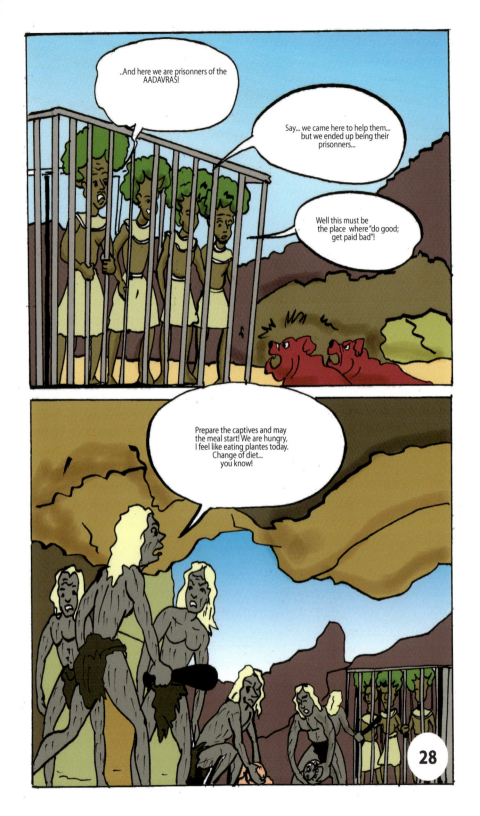

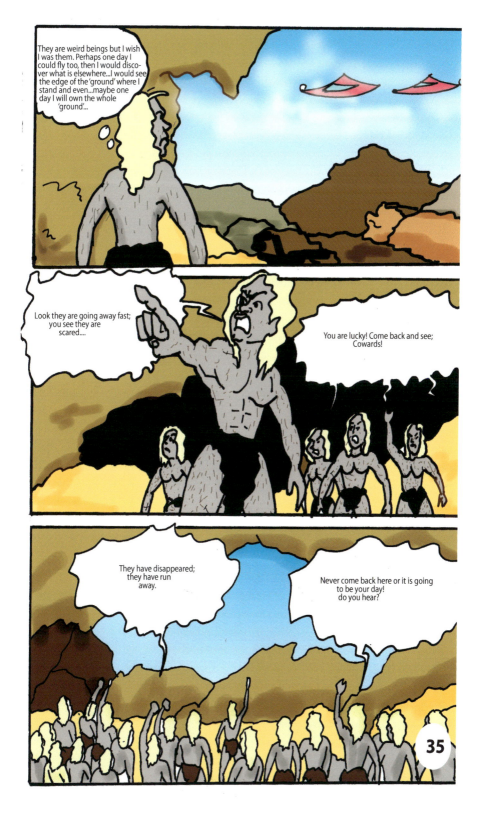

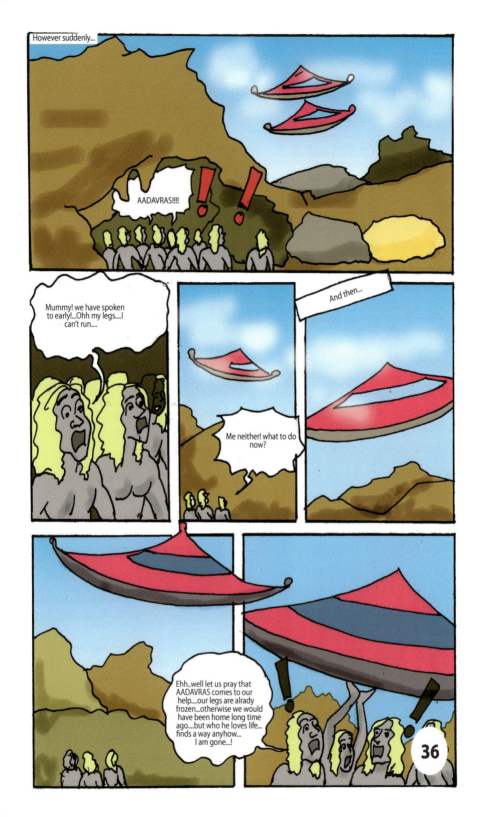

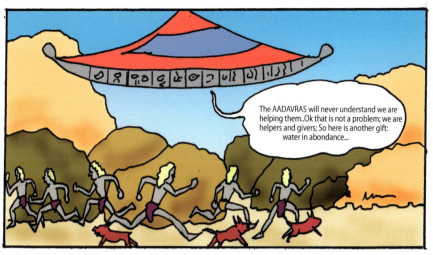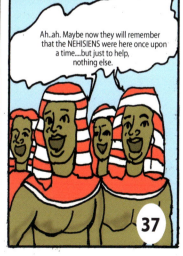

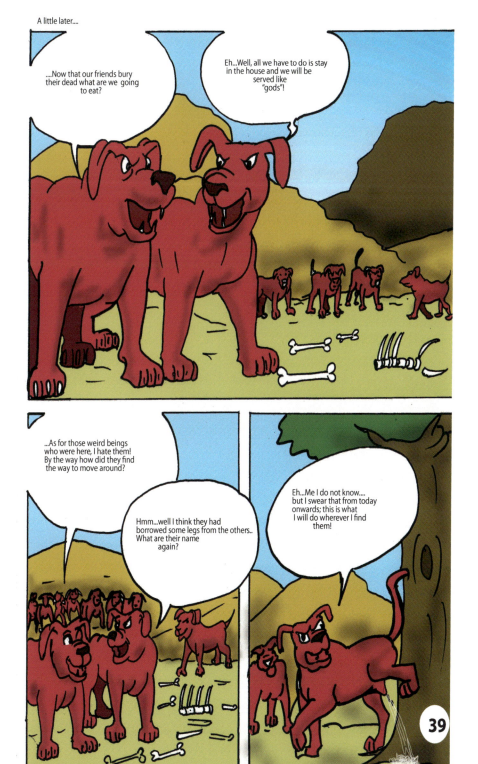

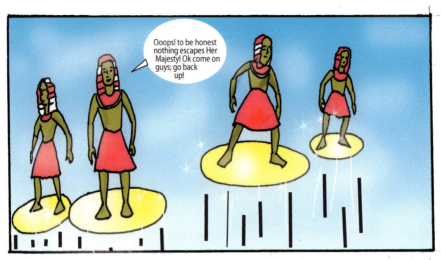

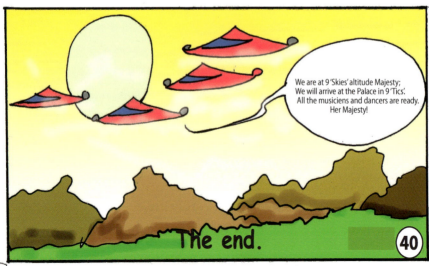

let's have some fun

The DJOSER Pyramid

See how quick you can fill the DJOSER pyramid with numbers. Add, take away, multiply or divide at **will** however making sure the equation correct.

Example:

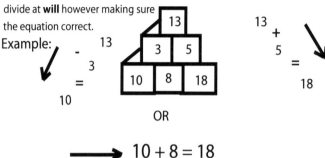

OR

➤ 10 + 8 = 18

Use 0 for all squares that cannot be used.

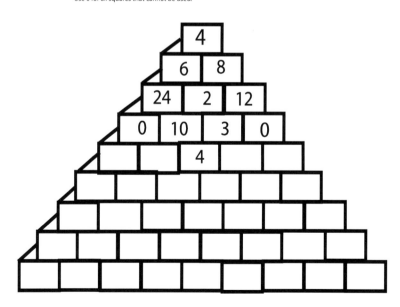

Symbolism

Can you see an ear and a mouth? or an African art object?

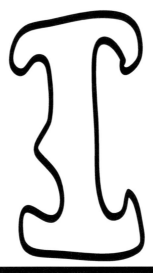

African...

Can you find all these countries in the grid?

Clues for directions:

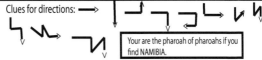

Your are the pharoah of pharoahs if you find NAMIBIA.

Benin
Sierra Leone
Zambia
Gambia
Togo
Ghana
Uganda
Mali
Eritree
Senegal
Zimbabwe
Libya
Togo
Tchad
Congo
Niger
Soudan
Kenya
Namibia
Nigeria
Azania (S.Africa)

```
S I E R R A L E O N E
E Z A M B T O G H A S
N A Z A I M A O . N W
E A I N A I L B . A A
G A M B I A T E N I Z
A . B L C K C S I N I
L Z A I O E H O G R L
E A B B N N A U E I A
R I W Y G Y D D R A N
T R E A O U G A N D D
```

42

Glossary And Explanation of Some Words And Names used In This Comic Book

AADAVRAS: 'Inhabitantants of the Carcass Mountain'.

AADAVRAS: God of the AADAVRAS

BAABUN: Baboon in Wolof, an African language spoken in West Africa.

BULLCHIEN: Created for the purpose of this Comic book;

CARCASS MOUNTAIN: Created for the purpose of this Comic book.

CROAAACH: Created for the purpose of this Comic book; chewin sound of the dinosaur bitting.

EARTHING: Created for the purpose of this Comic book; landing.

'GROUND': earth

HAJ: Created for the purpose of this Comic book; Dog in Wolof

MBAAM: In Wolof: Donkey.

MBELEE: In Wolof: Expression in Wolof ; Teased.

Miam: Created for the purpose of this Comic book; chewing sound.

NATURE: All the universes and what is in them.

NINE AIRES: Created for the purpose of this Comic book; distance 'equaling' thousands of miles wide.

NINE SKIES: Created for the purpose of this Comic book; distance 'equaling' thousands of mile up.

PAA RUWTY: African shero who could turna lioness or lion; Sphinx. PAA RUWTY-THE-LION-SPHINX.

POGS: Created for the purpose of this Comic book; an animal that is made up with many other animals.

REY: Pronounced RAY; from AMUN RE who was and still is an AFRICAN GOD. He was so great because he had the qualities of the SUN; being the MOST HIGH and GIVING LIFE. Today many simply say AMEN or AMIYN or AWMEN after their prayers.

SINDAH; Lezard in Wolof

SIX WINDS OR SIX AIRES: Created for the purpose of this Comic book; thousands of miles.

SUNS (FIVE): Created for the purpose of this Comic book; measure of time; equivalent of FIVE DAYS.

THREE, TWO STARS: Created for the purpose of this Comic book; directions.

TIC: Created for the purpose of this Comic book; equivalent of a split second.

WAF: Created for the purpose of this Comic book; sound of a dog barking.